Major Scale / Ionian Mod

Construction: whole step, whole step, half step, whole step, whole step, whole step, half step.

Use: with major chords and chords from the major family (major, 6th, maj. 7, maj. 9, add 9, 6/9).
Also, a major scale can be used with any chord in the major key. For example – use the C major scale with any of the chords in the key of C (C, Dm, Em, F, G, Am, and Bdim).

C Major

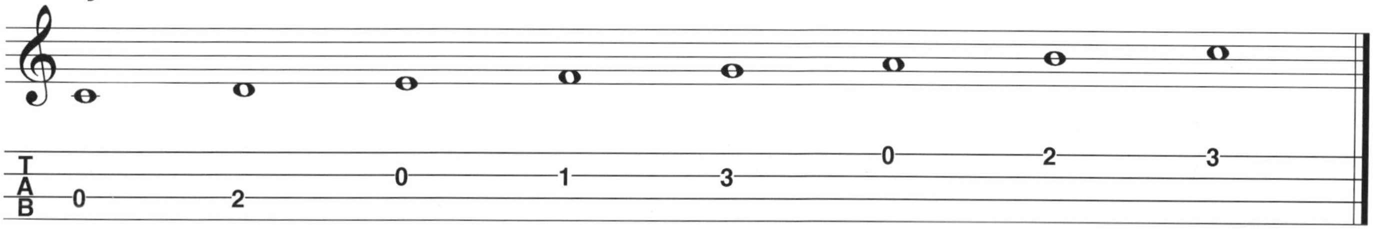

4th String Root ◆ = Root

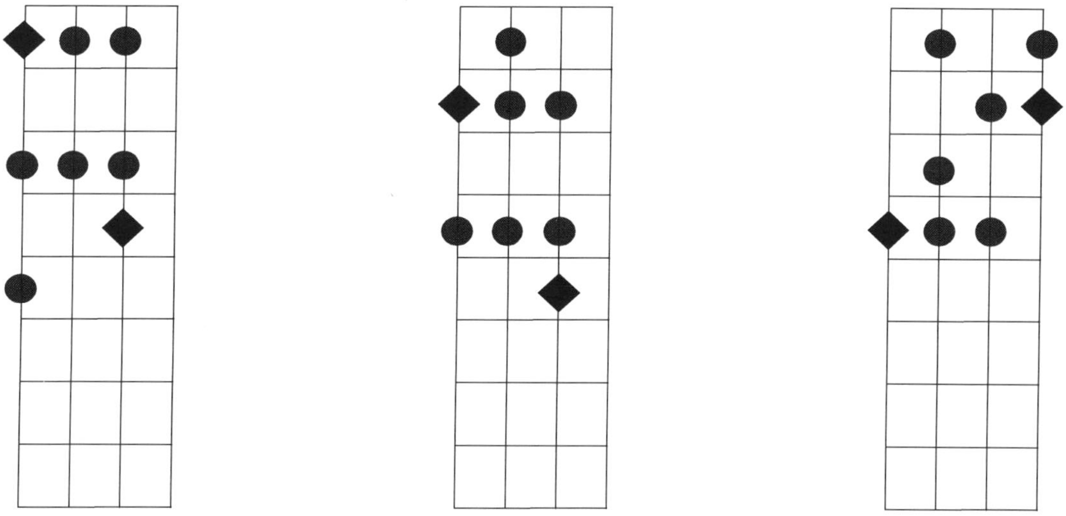

3rd String Root

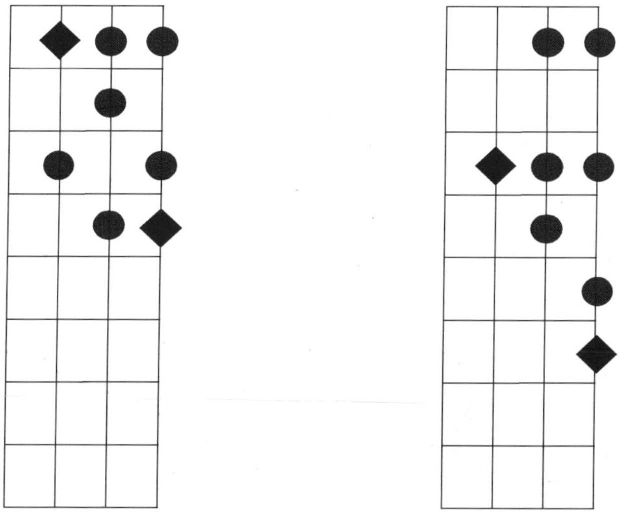

2nd String Root

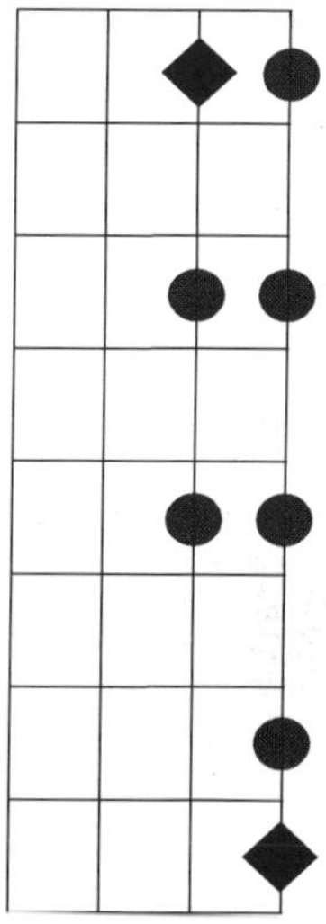

Natural Minor Scale / Aeolian Mode

Construction: major scale with a lowered 3rd, 6th, and 7th.

Use: with minor, m7, or m9 chords.

C Natural Minor

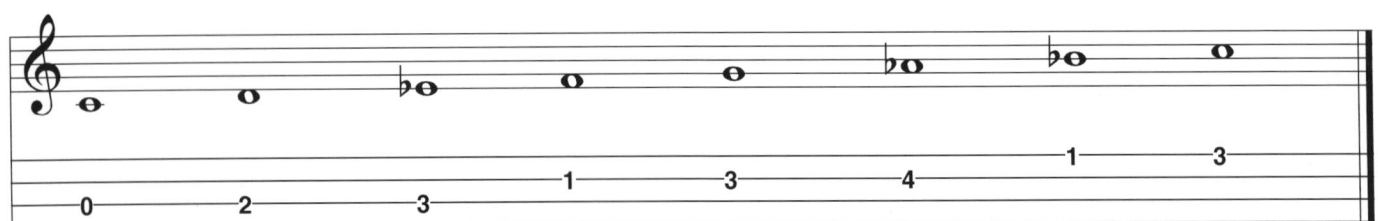

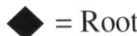

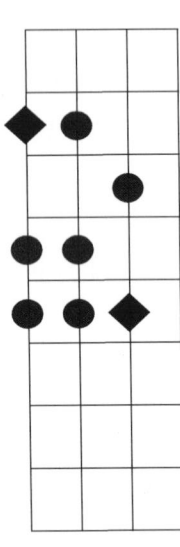

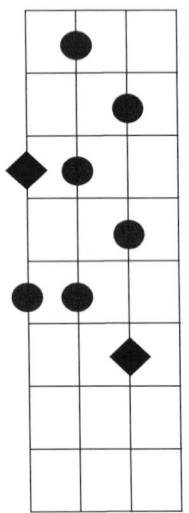

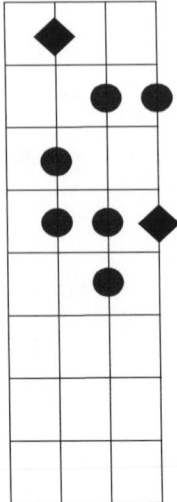

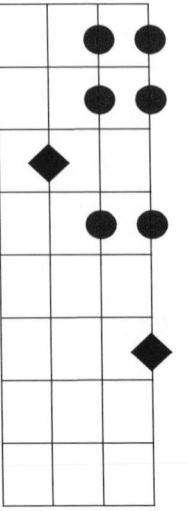

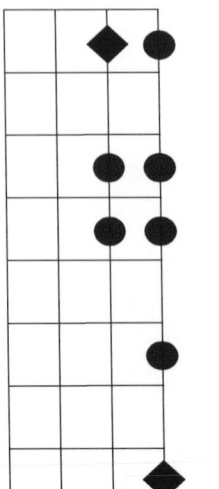

4

Harmonic Minor Scale

Construction: natural minor scale with a raised 7th.

Use: with minor, m7, m9, m+7, and other chords within a given minor key (A harmonic minor against Am, Bm7♭5, Dm, and E7)

C Harmonic Minor

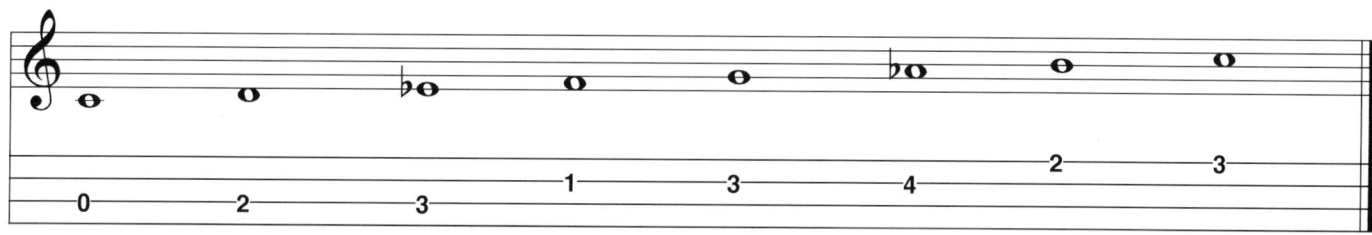

4th String Root

◆ = Root

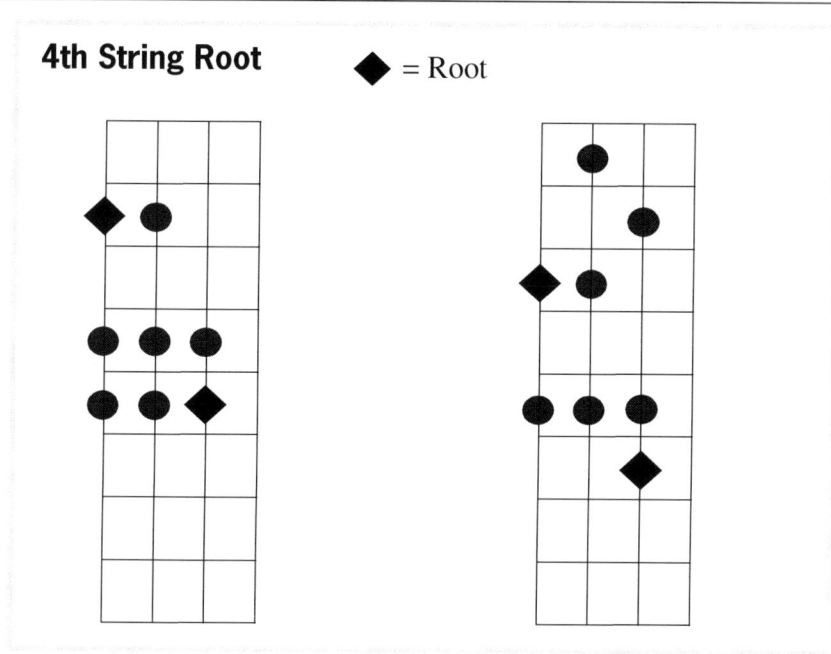

3rd String Root

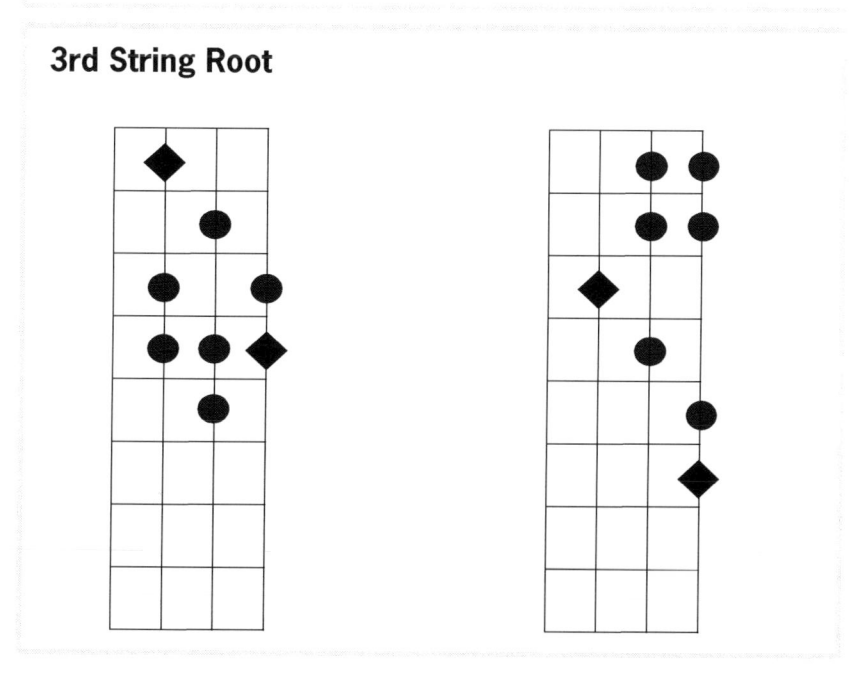

2nd String Root

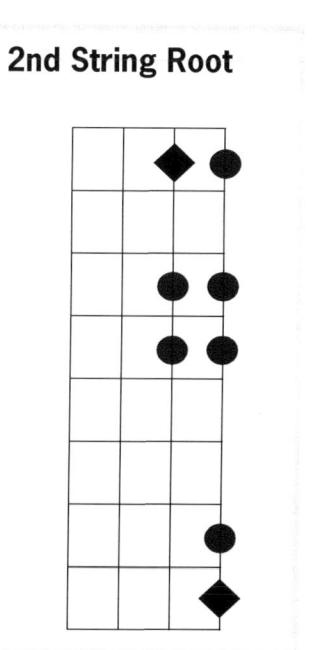

Melodic Minor Scale

Construction: natural minor scale with raised 6th and 7th degrees when ascending and not raised when descending (natural minor when descending).

Use: with minor type chords (minor, m6, m7, m+7, and m9) and other chords within a given minor key.

C Melodic Minor

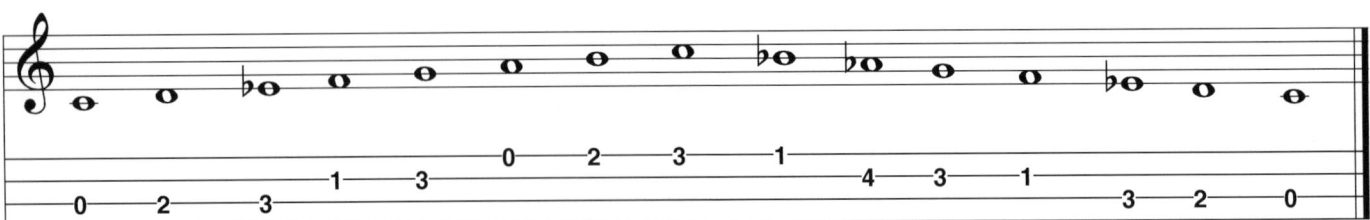

4th String Root
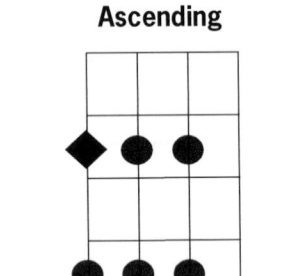

Ascending

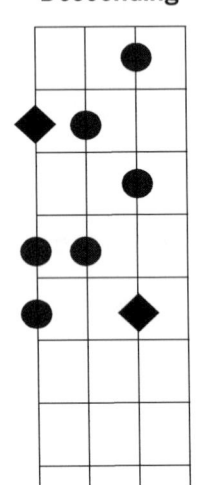

Descending

2nd String Root
Ascending

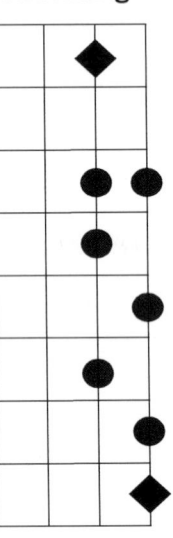

3rd String Root
Ascending

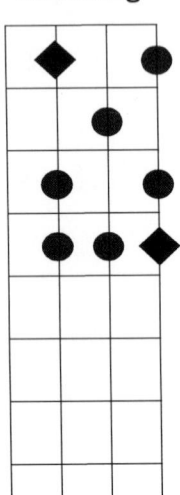

Descending

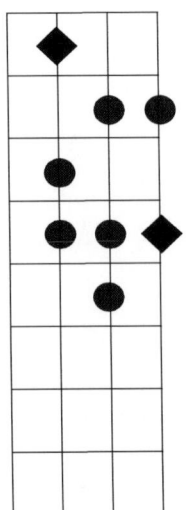

2nd String Root
Descending

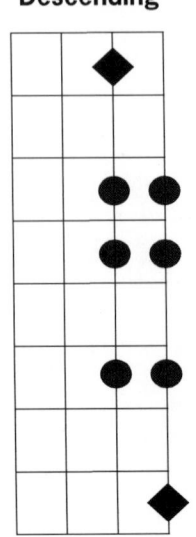

Major Pentatonic Scale

Construction: major scale with the half steps omitted (omitted 4th and omitted 7th).

Use: with major type chords (major, 6th, maj.7, maj. 9, add 9, and 6/9). Also, the major pentatonic scale can be used against a minor chord whose root is 1½ steps lower than the letter name of the major pentatonic scale.

C Major Pentatonic

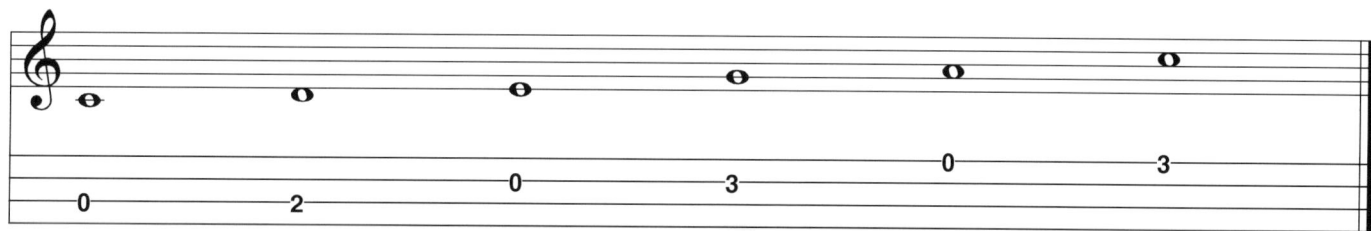

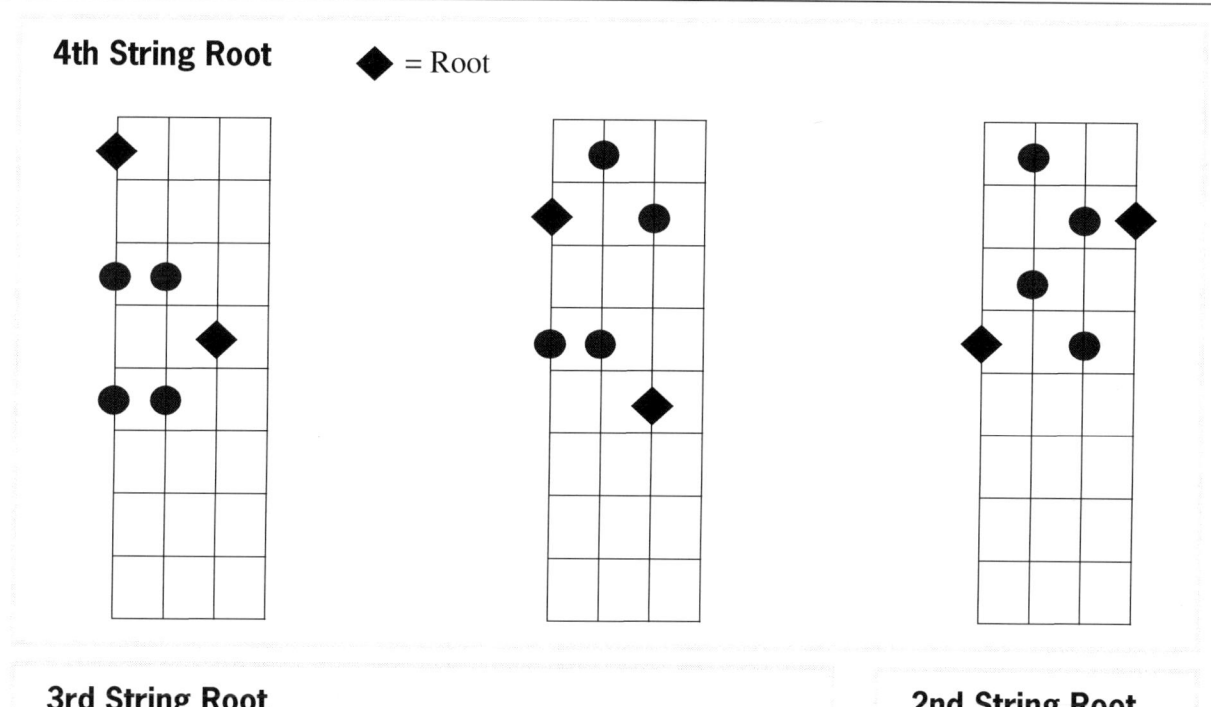

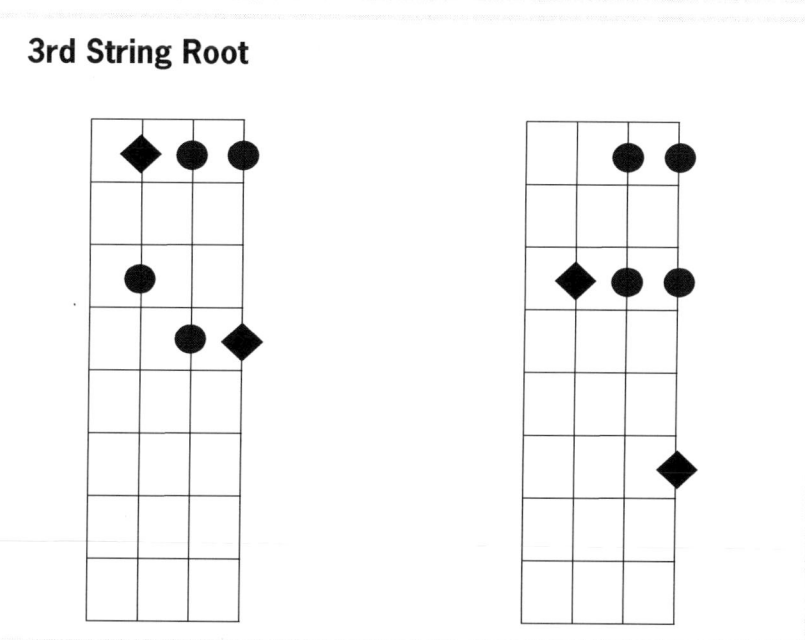

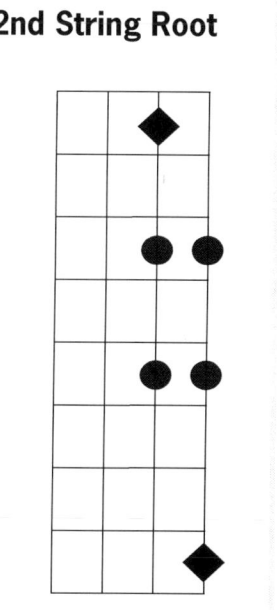

7

Minor Pentatonic Scale

Construction: natural minor scale with the half steps omitted (omitted 2nd and omitted 6th).

Use: with minor, m7, or m9 chords. Also, the minor pentatonic scale can be played against a major chord whose root is 1½ steps higher than the root of the minor pentatonic scale.

C Minor Pentatonic

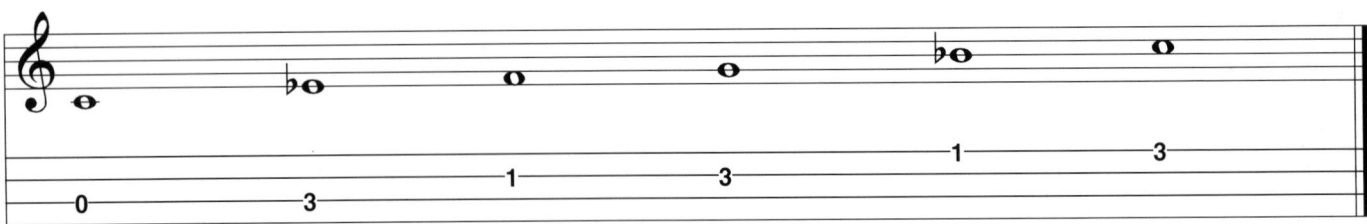

4th String Root   ◆ = Root

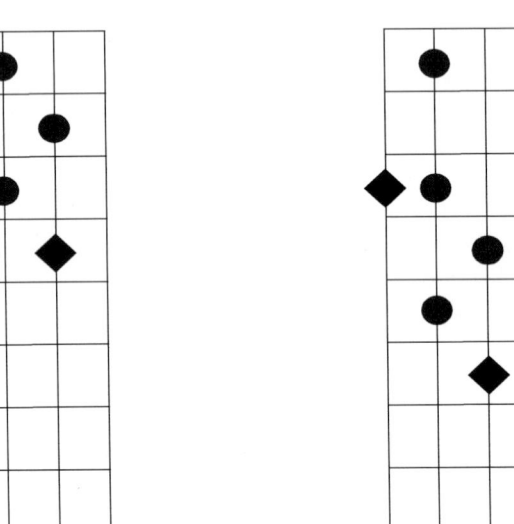

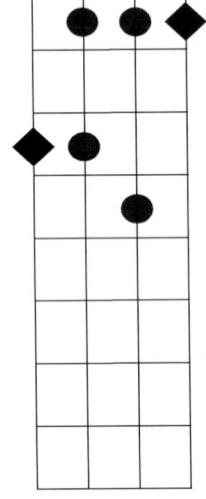

3rd String Root

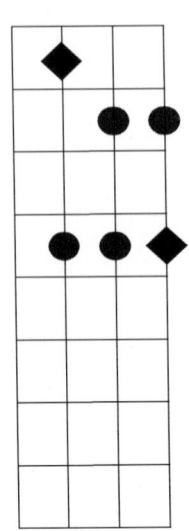

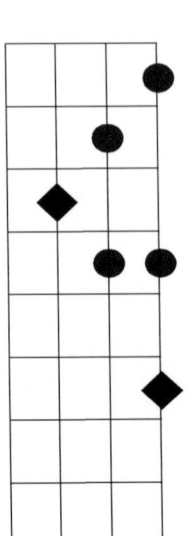

2nd String Root

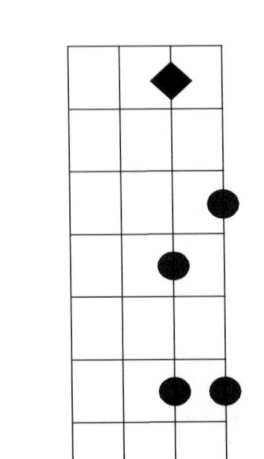

The Blues Scale

Construction: root, lowered 3rd, 4th, lowered 5th, natural 5th, and lowered 7th.

Use: with 7th, 9th, 11th, 13th, altered seventh chords (7♭5, 7♯9, etc.), or with any chord in the blues progression. The blues scale which is used should have the same letter name as the key in which the blues is being played. When the chords in the progression change, it is not necessary to change the scale.

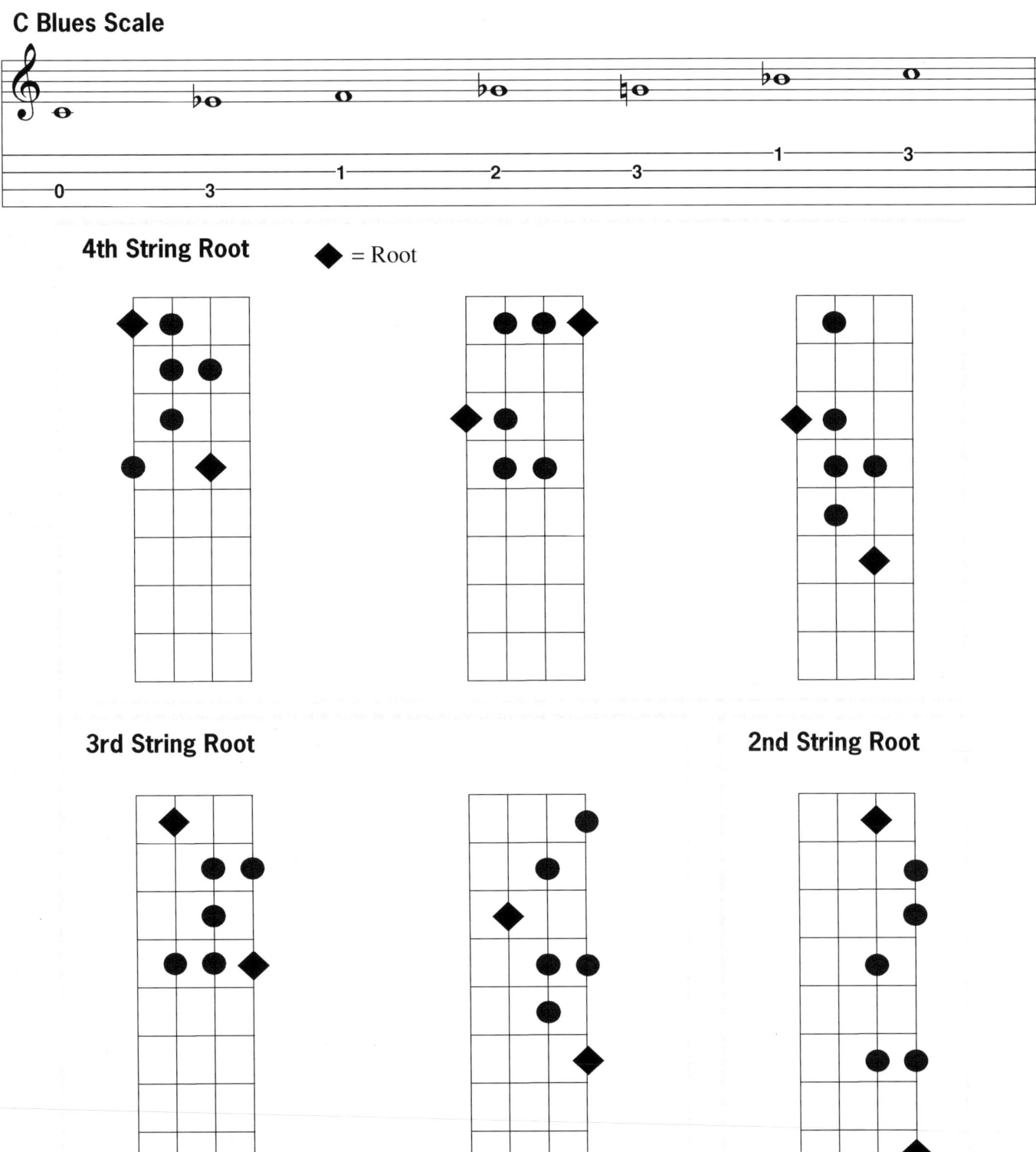

Dorian Mode

Construction: major scale beginning on the second degree (C dorian = B♭ major scale beginning on the C note).

Use: with minor, m6, m7, or m9 chords.

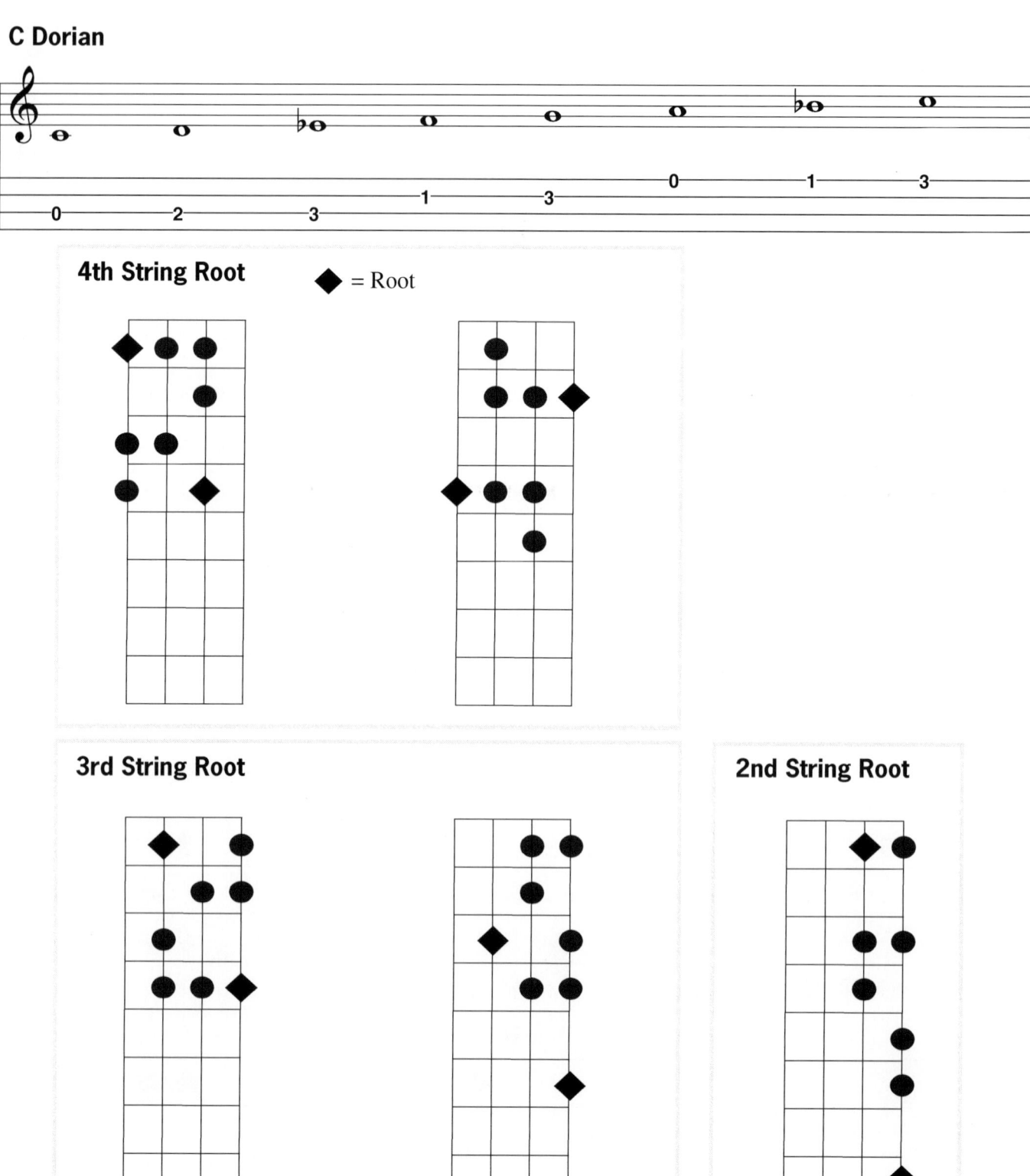

Mixolydian Mode

Construction: major scale beginning on the fifth degree (major scale with a lowered 7th).

Use: with 7th, 9th, 11th, and 13th chords.

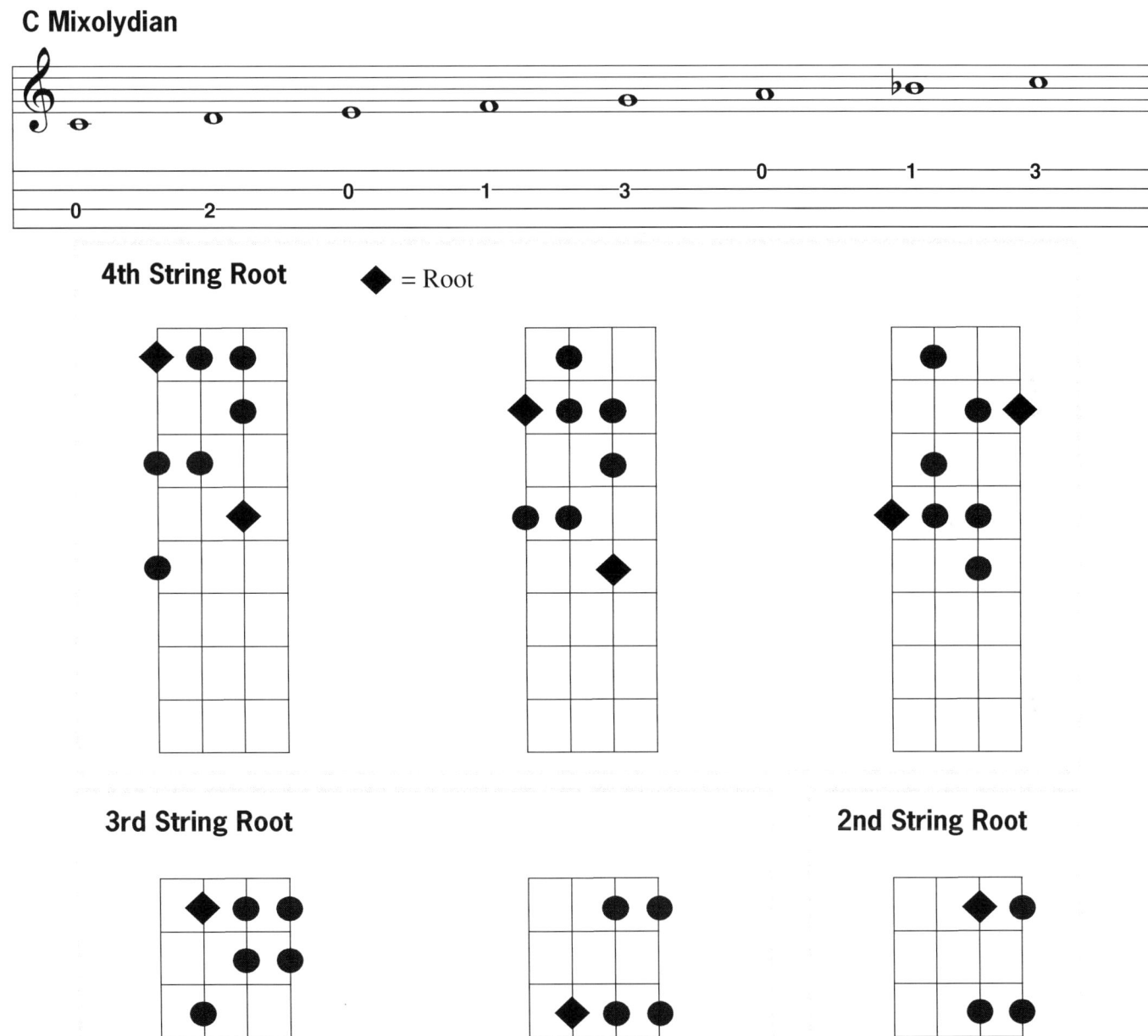

Phrygian Mode

Construction: major scale beginning on the third degree (E phrygian = C major scale beginning on the E note).

Use: with minor or m7 chords. To get a Spanish quality, the phrygian mode can also be played against a major chord (i.e., E phrygian against an E chord).

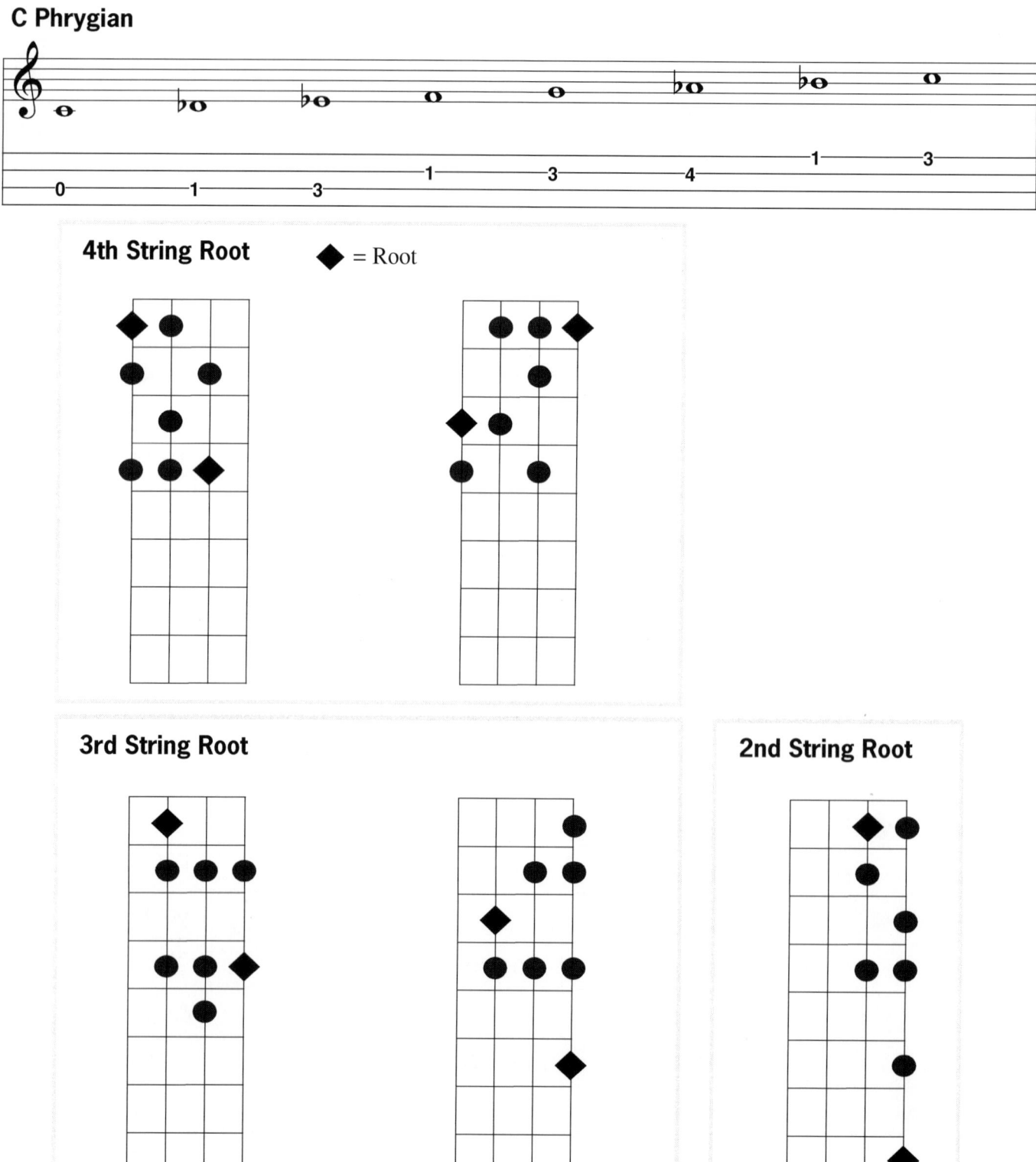

Diminished (Whole-Half)

Construction: whole-step, half-step, whole-step, half-step, etc.

Use: with diminished chords.

C Diminished (Whole-Half)

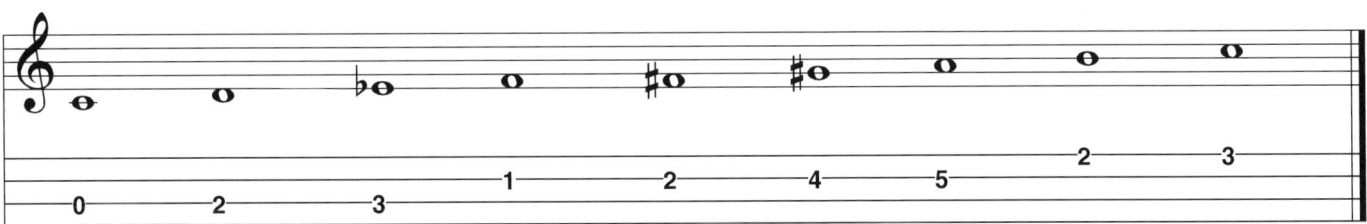

4th String Root

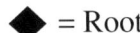 = Root

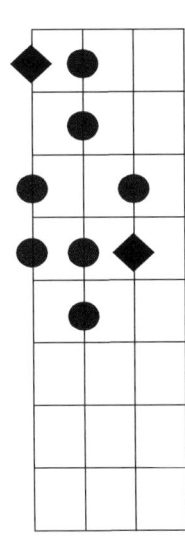

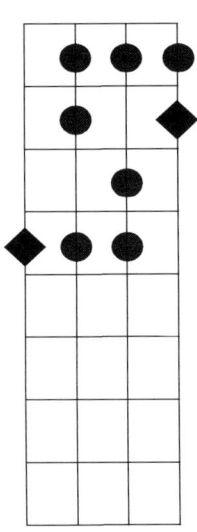

3rd String Root

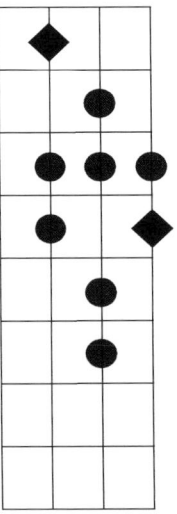

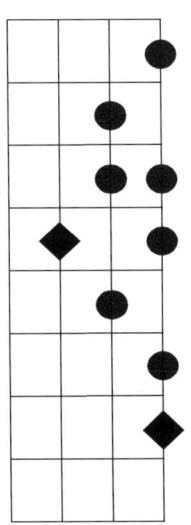

2nd String Root

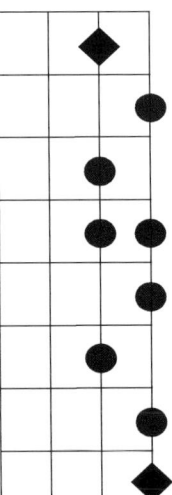

This scale book may be used for ukuleles in C tuning and D tuning. The only difference is the name of the note you would start on, depending on what fret you place the root note the scale name will change.

For example in C tuning the fourth string second fret is A, if you played the major scale pattern using A as the root note, you would be playing an A major scale. In D tuning the fourth string second fret is B if you played the major scale pattern using B as the root note, you would be playing an B major scale.

In C or D tuning the fingerings and patterns of the scales do not change, only the name (root note) of the scale. The scale fingerings are universal for both tunings.

Soprano Ukeleles

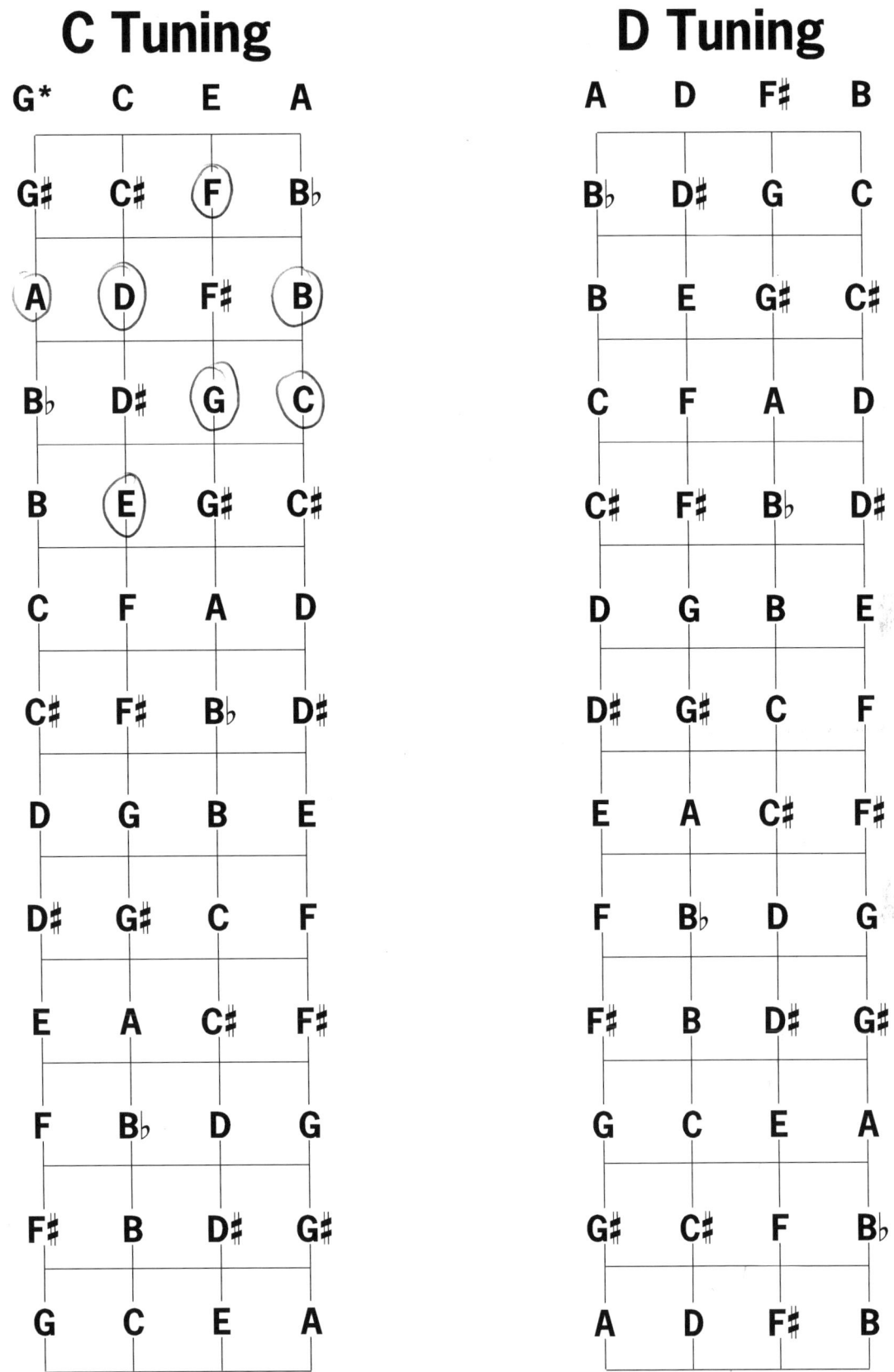

* G string may be tuned one octave lower, although a larger diameter string will be needed. This "Low G" tuning is common for tenor ukeleles.